Angel Whispers

written and illustrated by
Michelle V. Whalley

RoseDog 🐾 Books

PITTSBURGH, PENNSYLVANIA 15222

For information or to order additional books, please write:
RoseDog Books
701 Smithfield St.
Pittsburgh, PA 15222
U.S.A.
1-800-834-1803
Or visit our web site and
on-line bookstore at www.rosedogbookstore.com

Full size copies of illustrations in *Angel Whispers* are available.
Please contact RoseDog Books for more information.

Heartfelt Dedication...

...to my friend who now lives with her angels and who inspired me to attempt, as well as to keep going with this book.

...to Klara, my granddaughter, a very new soul in this universe and an angel in her own way.

...to Momma and my Dad.

...to angels everywhere.

Deep Appreciation...

...to my husband, Harold, who lovingly puts up with me on a daily basis. ("It works both ways," he says.)

...to Debbie, without whom I would still be typing out the first poem and there would be nothing yet to edit.

...to Fran, who predicted from the start that there would be over one hundred angels and who has helped me edit in "crunch" times.

...to Sue and Pat, who previewed my work as I went along and through their feedback encouraged me to continue.

...to Jean, John, Jane, Diane and Joyce, who encouraged me to publish.

...to Marge and her daughter, Diane, who kept me accountable and forward moving.

...to Trey and Monika, Tim and Wanda, Kelly, Stephen and Jackie, Phil and Ginny, Joan, Myra, Ellen, Elisa, Nona and Rene, Katie and Nick, Deidre and Anthony, Jessica and Arty, Meg, Melissa, Adam, Chrissy, Eloine, Jackie and Greg, Mary-Ellen, and all who supported, encouraged and believed in me and this book.

...to angels everywhere.

Prologue

Dear Reader,

Hello! Welcome to my book...

I have always believed that there are angels and just when I might have a doubt...wham! There they are!

Angels for me are everywhere. They are in a breeze's whisper, a stranger's words, the twilight hush of a day's end and so forth. It is a truly individual experience. Oftentimes, in my life, I have been comforted, helped, guided and, yes, even hugged by what I believe have been angels: human and ethereal.

I started drawing these angels in July of 1999, shortly after my mother Clara's passing. In my mind, I saw Michaelangelo's and Reuben's angels but here were these "cartoons" coming out of my hand! There was an intense need to draw them and I was "driven." These drawings came with their own "titles" or their own "names." One drawing came with the title "Life H20 Emergency." I questioned, "How presumptuous? Wouldn't it be easier to just call it 'Drought'?" No, it was to be "Life H2O Emergency." That made me laugh. For "cartoons" they appeared to have their very own soul and message.

During that same period of time, I had a friend who was very ill. She, too, believed in angels and had experienced them in different ways throughout her life. We felt that we were to publish a children's book of angel poems and pictures together. She would write the poems and I would illustrate them. However, before that could occur, she crossed over.

I was compelled to continue drawing these angel pictures. There presently are well over 200 of them and they are all very different, yet similar. I have written poems for many of them.

While these drawings, with their "titles," come seemingly out of the blue and often surprise me, their "titles" have provided a guide to my writing the poems that come from my heart. Their messages have an appeal to the child in all of us. These messages have brought me peace, made my heart smile and, sometimes, have made me sad.

If you choose to take this book home with you, may they do the same for you.

May angels be ever with you.

Sincerely,
Michelle Veilleux Whalley

Angel Whispers

Angel whispers are all around
And in all directions do abound.
They are there for us to hear.
Angel whispers lift our souls and calm our fears.
You have to listen for them though
but once you hear them,
you'll always know.

They come to you regardless that your skies are sunny.
Angel whispers help you laugh when life is less than honey.
They protect and guide you with words that you know
Like..."be careful", think twice" and "go for it-go!"
You have to listen for them though
but once you hear them,
you'll always know.

While angel whispers oftentimes are quiet,
They can also be loud and intense,
Especially if you're caught in a riot
Or catch your pants going over a fence.
You have to listen for them though
but once you hear them,
you'll always know.

When there is danger and you might be hurt,
Angel whispers can be sharp and curt
Though they always come to you with love...
With love in their words as soft as a dove.
You have to listen for them though
but once you hear them,
you'll always know.

So listen carefully as you live.
Angel whispers are there always to give
Needed guidance and protection
In your moments of reflection.

You have to listen for them though
but once you hear them,
you'll always know.

Believe

Believe in all that you can see
The land... the stream... the giving tree.

Believe in all that you can feel
A rock... some silk... an oily eel.

Believe in all that you can hear
The wind... a bird's song... a "noisy" deer.

Believe in those you know who care
About truth and love and being fair.

Believe all that is good and all that is true
The Present... the Future... and the "not so new."

Believe in what you cannot see
Whose whispers say "Come follow me."

And in doing all this, you'll never lose your way
In a life that is wrought with many turns
That sometimes leave one with hurt and burns.

But most importantly of all, believe in the One
Who turns night into day and lights up the sun.

Beach Rose

There is an angel named Beach Rose
Who travels from coast to coast.
She watches over sailors
And makes the fish french toast.

She has a sense of humor
As she travels on her waves.
She sets out funny rumors
And drops them in seacaves
To make the crayfish laugh and rail
And tickle the funny bones of whales.

She loves to jump upon the sea
And set the lobsters in traps free.
She plays a seaweed harpsichord
For all the fish to hear.
When the bass are scared or bored,
She entertains them and removes their fear.

Beach Rose is never seen by man
But one will know she's near...
For amid the smell of salty brine
Rose's scent is very clear.

So when you smell roses at the beach,
Remember, keep your toes out of her reach
For she will tickle them 'til you cry out,
"Time out, Rose...time out!"

Want To Come With Me?

Want to come with me?
Oh, the wonderful things that we could do and see!

Do you know what an iceberg looks like...on the inside?
Have you ever traveled through a humongous riptide?

We could slide down a brilliant and shiny rainbow
Or find an old Polynesian warship that we could row.

Can you think of how many hairs grow on the back of a yak?
If you were tiny enough, you'd get lost walking on its back.

But don't be scared, as I would be with you.
Ever here to guide and protect you.

Want to come with me?
Oh, the wonderful things we could hear and could see!

We could go to the tippety top of the world
Where we could see clouds...all of them swirled.

While there we could listen to the winds of the centuries.
Or we could simply sit on our knees in a garden of peas.

We could go to the crests of the mountains
Where volcanoes make fountains of lava,
Then stop at a café for a hot mocha java.

Oh, the wonderful things we could hear, feel and see,
If you were to just come with me.

Wash Day

Scrub-a-dub-dub
Four wings in the tub
Two wings on the line
So things will be fine.

Soon we will be going
To Earth on a trip
To help Sarah with sowing
And Adam in doing a "flip."

Sarah works hard planting in the dirt.
Adam does his "flips" in mud and might just get hurt.
So both are dirty jobs
But someone has to do it!

Our wings will soil
With all of this "toil."
So what can I say?
Another wash day!

The Magic of a Puddle

Have you ever looked into a puddle?
Do you know that you have to get down
... and lean very close
... to see what it holds?

When you do though...
You'll be so very surprised...
For there in that puddle
...is a wonderful teeny-tiny world.
Did I say teeny-tiny world?
Well, it really depends on the size of the puddle.
It can be a small world...
Or it can be a humongous world...
...especially when you're only three feet tall.

The sky, the houses, the trees and more
Can be seen in this watery carpet
...on the Earth's lowly floor.

Sometimes, there are very small inhabitants
...in this watery world.
A skimmer bug?
A water worm?
An ant on a raft?

And sometimes...very big ones!
Look at your face in this moisture place.
What do you see when you look?
...a giant?
...a king?
...a happy face?

Oh, the magic of a puddle!

Clyde Cat

Clyde Cat is an angel,
An angel only for cats,
And though there's no angle
He is exactly just that.

Everyone knows a cat has nine lives
And that we have but just one.
So Clyde has nine times more to give
Each cat before his job is done.

He is there with his cats
As they go through nine coats.
He wears many hats
But none of them float.

So when one of his cats
Goes in for a swim,
They go at their own risk
And they go without him.

He flies, though, above them
And coaches them on
Until they reach the shore
And the danger is gone.

Clyde Cat is an angel
An angel for cats
And quite simply,
That is just that!

Crazy Day

Have you ever had a crazy day?
One when all just goes awry...
You're wearing plaid with polka dots
And your pants' hems are just too high?

The bus is late.
Your mother's cross.
You break a plate.
Your cat is lost.

These days, also, happen to angels.
Eliza's day was like that once.
Her gown of yellow, in the wash,
Had turned the brightest pink.

Her halo sprouted flowers
And turned into a hat.
Her silken wings had polka dotted
Developing a most peculiar stink!

"Oh well," she thought most seriously,
"I'll have to work like this."
However, as she went about her way
Her wings began to hiss.
"Oh no!" she thought deliriously,
"I cannot fly like this."

So, she took her wings off
To quickly wash
But there was no soap to find.
Then she said, "This is all just in my mind!"

"My attitude is off the wall,
With all of this dismay.
I just have to stand up tall
And face this crazy day."

So Eliza took a deep breath in,
Then squared away her shoulders
And made the rest of her crazy day
... a day for moving boulders.

Jude

When there is something that can't be "dood"
And you're pulling out your hair
Just call out the name of a man named Jude
And you'll no longer know that care.

The impossible to us
Is commonplace to him.
So when things are in a "muss"
He'll come in to quiet the din.

The many times stonewalls "pop" out of the ground
And stop you in your shoes
Jude will take those walls right down
As if he did it in a "snooze."

You see, he does the impossible
And that is his expertise.
So when things seem not "do-able,"
He'll fix them in a sneeze.

Remember always to say please and thank you,
For manners are very good
To use with the man in this line of work...
A man who is known as Jude.

So Many Roads to Travel
So Many Paths to Follow
(My Child's Angel Speaks)

So many roads to travel,
So many paths to follow,
I'll be pounding the gravel
Through tomorrows after tomorrow.

It's my job to guide him
As he journeys through this life,
To answer all his questions
And protect him from any strife.

He has to listen to me though
As he often feels he can do it alone.
And when he on the wrong path goes,
He seeks my help with a mighty groan.

I know with aging and with "mileage"
That he will mellow
And use my help to avoid life's "garbage"...
As he truly is a good-souled fellow.

We'll follow God's light
As we travel his way.
It will always burn bright
To guide us each day.

I like my job as we "get around"
And travel over all kinds of ground.
So many roads to travel...
We'll both enjoy pounding the gravel!

P.S. God bless you always! Love, Mom

The Night Shift

As light of day fades
and dark begins to lift...
The time becomes that...
of the angels' night shift.
Little ones in miniature shrouds
emerge and descend from all of the clouds.
They come to Earth...
to guard us here
And though not seen...
are always near...
To wake a mother to her infant's cry
To wipe a tear from a frightened child's eye
To hold an elder's hand...
through the night's veiled tears
And now and then to whisper...
into one's ears
that all will be well
...though the night is so dark,
That God's love will hold one...
until dawn's breaking light
when the day angels come
and take over their place,
As the night shift leaves
to allow the day's pace
To be guided by these.

Procession

In the early dawning hours
As you look into the skies,
Watch the "twinkles" as they go soaring
And you won't believe your eyes.

You'll say that it's your eye wrinkling
That just made the light "go that way"
But it's millions of little angels twinkling
While on their way to pray.

They're going back from the nightshift,
Having guarded you through this time.
All the prayers emitting from their lips
Fill the sky with angel rhyme.

They carry each a candle
Whose light flickers as they drift.
These flickers cause the "twinkles"
That our eyes see as they lift.

These flickers that cause the "twinkles"
Have burned throughout the night
To protect us from those spirits
That would not do us right.

How special you are, you know,
To have witnessed this nightly recession
As the angels eternally come and go
Continuing their daily processions.

Angelrise

In the early morning twilight,
That time that's in-between,
The air is damp with night
The light is very lean.

The quiet is astounding...
A great humongous hush.
That's the time of angelrise
When there is nothing in a rush.

Not a word is spoken.
The mistiness is near.
The movement of wings is silent.
Yet, if you listen, you can hear
The whispers, sighs and rustle
Of some other worldly beings.

The talk is of the day to come
And of all the work that must be done.
The joy, the anger and the sorrow
The talk of this tomorrow
That is dawning ever near.

Soon, the light will brighten.
The night will wash away.
The air will sweetly lighten

... for angelrise is here!

Only One

Although on this Earth most things come by twos,
There are some that come only one.
There is only one angel who is just for you.
There is only one moon and one sun.
There is only the One who made this Earth,
Who set forth the night and the day,
Who sent us our angel, who gives us mirth,
And created the Milky Way.
He is known by many, many names.
Yaweh, Jehovah, and God are but some.
But each of these names causes mankind great pain
As he struggles to establish the One.
He does not seem to be clear
That these many are really but One.
And that possible thought seems to cause great fear,
Fear that someone else's God just might...
Might be the One that is true.
And this he does fight...
Fight that he's right...
Just trying to fill that One shoe.
But there is truly only One,
And if we could all find one common name,
There would be Peace here on Earth
And all would know His worth

...as the same!

Have You Ever Seen a Miracle?

Have you ever seen a miracle?
I have everyday that I have looked for one.
Miracles do not have to be lyrical.
You'll know them by the light of the moon or the sun.

Look at the small flower growing
In a desert, without ever knowing
That it should not be able
To grow...without rain or a watertable.

Watch the bumblebee that flies between the flowers.
It truly defies all aviational powers.
That lets us know that impossible things flow
Throughout this life that we know.

Listen to an infant's cry as he is born
In either a palace or a site forlorn.
It tells us that life will continue along
Regardless of what is right or what is wrong.

It never ceases to amaze me
When I stop and listen or look
That there are ever so many miracles.
They could just fill books...and books!

Monika's Garden

Monika's garden is grown from love
And all who visit there will hear the dove
That lives in the tree and sings heartfelt songs.

Songs which take one away from the everyday throngs,
Who stomp upon the world's flowers (as well as the weeds)
And in doing that, interfere with the needs...
That give us all life.

Our tears of joy and tears of grief...
They water what grows in this lovely place
Where time flows at a slower pace.

We each need that place...
... A place to hang our hat
... A place to put our feet up
... A place to have a lovely chat,
While we drink from summer's cup
Of love... and peace... and life...
Where we can all be free of strife
... in Monika's garden.

Faith

Faith is an ever-changing being.
It can be as strong as a mountain
Or as fragile as a butterfly's wing.
It can fill up an entire rocket.
It can fit into a pocket.
It can allow you to challenge
A den full of dragons.

If faith is sparse, you just might wail
With the anguished shout of an injured snail.

Answers are so hard to find.
People often lose their mind
As they seek to know the why.
Day after day they often try
But not all answers are to be given.
So, the Lord must be forgiven.

However, He, always, has His reasons
And so, He gives us faith to carry us
Throughout life's tumultuous seasons.

There is one thing though that is for certain,
The more that you have,
The more that it grows
From the top of your head
To the tips of your toes.

So feel it fill you each time you renew.
Hold on to it tight
As it might be a fight
To hold on to this treasure
That gives one such pleasure.

Always remember that
Faith can tear apart strife
As you pass through this wonder-filled life.

So, find your faith,
Keep your faith,
And let it grow!

Requiem

Requiem is a very sad song
That always seems so black and forlorn.
Yet, if one steps away from the thought of the throngs,
One will hear Gabriel's most joyous horn.

The "rest in peace" is truly true,
For Abba's hand
Is the place for you
To achieve this peace in a Blessed Land.

Tears fall for the loneliness
That the living feel,
But the entire quiescence
Is one with appeal.

To the one who has happened to cross,
The reunion with loved ones
Is most wonderful, never again to be lost,
For the soul is now free of all pain and of shun.

So, when Requiem comes into your life,
Be happy for the person who is now without strife.
And know that the moment it happens to you,
You will know joy and peace... through and through.

Slay or Slice and Share

In days of old
When knights were bold
There was an order each day
For a dragon to slay.

Now George would kill dragons
And then drink his flagons
To celebrate his gains,
But all the dragons ever felt... was most severe pain.

The fact of the matter
Was George just got fatter.
The dragon's numbers diminished
Until George was finished.

But Michael was fairer
In his slaying of dragons.
They at least had a prayer for staying alive.

Michael only slew
Those that were evil
And so his numbers were fewer than few.
With those that were good,
He would slice and share food.

So slay or slice and share?
What would one do
When faced with a choice
That should be fair?

What would you do?

House of Life

There is a place called the House of Life.
It sits at the bottom of a hill.
Those who go there know no strife
As all is very still.

The peace found there
Refreshes your soul.
As one breathes in the air,
The essence makes one whole.

Healing is the purpose
For this House of Life.
Anything you might want or wish
Is right there in your sight.

Peace and love and harmony
Are packaged up as gifts.
Sunny skies are many
To minimize your drift.

The angel at this House of Life will lovingly care
For just you, as you visit there.
She'll tend your soul and give you peace
As you stay and share.

Yo! Wait a Minute!

Yo! Wait a minute!
Have I got a message for you!
Today they have a special
On Irish Mulligan stew.

The bowls are two
For the price of one.
So I'll go with you
And we'll have some fun.

Yo! Wait a minute!
We'll catch up on how your life's been going,
While we drink from a coffee cup
And watch the traffic flowing.

Yo! Wait a minute!
You know life's been going too fast for you
And it's time to do some slowing.
So you and I can stop for stew
While I help you with your growing.

Yo! Wait a minute!

Boo! I see you...I'm here

When life feels sad and very gray
If you listen closely...you will hear me say,
Boo! I see you...I'm here.

When you're at a life's crossroads
Deciding how to best juggle its loads,
Boo! I see you...I'm here.

When you're in a place with vicious crocodiles
That can take away your very last smiles,
Boo! I see you...I'm here.

When your heart is truly broken
And you think you really don't give a token,
Boo! I see you...I'm here.

When you're sick and your fever blazes
And you no longer see anyone's loving gazes,
Boo! I see you...I'm here.

When life makes you delirious
With all its varied "mysterious",
Boo! I see you...I'm here.

It is at these times...when you least expect
a helping hand or a word of praise,
that "Boo!" will come to show you a way.
For Boo! means, "I'm here!
I'll help!
I'll carry your worry.
The day is bright...so don't you hurry!"